Spot the Difference

# Stems

## Charlotte Guillain

Heinemann Library
Chicago, Illinois

P9-ELO-538

© 2008 Heinemann Library
a division of Capstone Global Libraray, LLC.
Chicago, Illinois

Customer Service 800-747-4992
Visit our website at www.heinemannraintree.com

All rights reserved. No part of this publication may be reproduced or transmitted in any form or by any means, electronic or mechanical, including photocopying, recording, taping, or any information storage and retrieval system, without permission in writing from the publisher.

Designed by Joanna Hinton-Malivoire
Photo research by Erica Martin and Hannah Taylor
Printed in the United States of America in Eau Claire, Wisconsin.
012014  007962RP

**Library of Congress Cataloging-in-Publication Data**
Guillain, Charlotte.
  Stems / Charlotte Guillain. -- 1st ed.
    p. cm. -- (Spot the difference)
  Includes index.
  ISBN-13: 978-1-4329-0943-7
  ISBN-10: 1-4329-0943-6
  ISBN-13: 978-1-4329-0950-5
  ISBN-10: 1-4329-0950-9
  1.  Stems (Botany)--Juvenile literature.  I. Title.
  QK646.G85 2008
  581.4'95--dc22
                          2007035950

**Acknowledgements**
The publishers would like to thank the following for permission to reproduce photographs: ©FLPA pp.**14**, **22 right** (Chris Mattison), **6**, **17** (Nigel Cattlin), **11**, **23b** (Silvestris Fotoservice); ©Getty Images p.**10** (Photographer's Choice/Grant Faint); ©istockphoto.com pp.**4 bottom right** (Stan Rohrer), **4 top left** (CHEN PING-HUNG), **4 top right** (John Pitcher), **15**, **23 top** (rion819), **4 bottom left** (Vladimir Ivanov); ©Nature picture library pp.**20** (Jason Ingram), **13** (Philippe Clement); ©Photolibrary pp.**8** (Image Source Limited), **16** (Botanica /Sklar Evan), **19** (Jason Ingram), **7** (Michael Diggin), **9**, **22** left (Pacific Stock), **21** (Plainpicture Gmbh & Co Kg), **18** (Susie Mccaffrey); ©Science photo library pp.**5** (Adam Jones), **12** (Maria & Bruno Petriglia).

Cover photograph of sunflowers reproduced with permission of ©Science Photo Library (Jeff Lepore). Back cover photograph of a strawberry runner reproduced with permission of ©Photolibrary (Botanica /Sklar Evan).

Every effort has been made to contact copyright holders of any material reproduced in this book. Any omissions will be rectified in subsequent printings if notice is given to the publishers.

# Contents

# What Are Plants?

Plants are living things.
Plants live in many places.

Plants need air to grow.
Plants need water to grow.
Plants need sunlight to grow.

# What Are Stems?

flower

leaf

stem

roots

Plants have many parts.

Most plants have stems.

# Different Stems

stem

This is a buttercup.
Its stem is short.

This is a sunflower.
Its stem is long.

stem

This is a redwood tree.
Its stem is thick.

This is a bean plant.
Its stem is thin.

This is a burnet.
It has one stem.

This is lavender.
It has many stems.

# Amazing Stems

spike

This is a cactus.
Its stem has thin spikes.

This is a rose.
Its stem has thick spikes.

stem

This is a strawberry plant.
Its stem grows along the ground.

This is an ivy plant.
Its stem grows along other plants.

This is a dogwood plant.
Its stem is red.

This is a golden willow.
Its stem is yellow.

# What Do Stems Do?

Stems hold leaves above the ground.

Stems carry water to the leaves.

# Spot the Difference!

How many differences can you see?

# Index

**Note to Parents and Teachers**

**Before reading**
Talk to the children about the stems of plants. Show them a flower and ask them what different things grow on the stem (leaves, flowers). Explain that stems are very different for different plants. The stem of a tree is its trunk.

**After reading**
• Ask the children to tell you all the different things that they have learned about stems. Make a list of their suggestions. Give out some plant catalogs and ask the children to look through them and find pictures which show the stem of a plant. They should cut these out and make a collage.  Help them to label the stems and add any information that they told you.
• Place a celery stalk which has some leaves in a jar. Make 4 slits in the bottom of the stalk. Fill the jar halfway with water. Add red food coloring. Watch the leaves of the celery stalk change color.

# Picture Glossary

**spike**  a sharp point

**stem**  the part of a plant that holds it up. Stems also carry water.